Exploring Earth and Space

Objects in the Sky

Rachel Hudson

PowerKiDS press™

NEW YORK

Published in 2013 by The Rosen Publishing Group, Inc.
29 East 21st Street, New York, NY 10010

Book Design: Michael Harmon

Photo Credits: Cover Korionov/Shutterstock.com; p. 4 David De Lossy/Thinkstock.com; p. 5 (sun) Stockbyte/Thinkstock.com; pp. 5 (moon), 7 iStockphoto/Thinkstock.com; p. 6 © iStockphoto.com/loops7; p. 8 Digital Vision./Thinkstock.com; p. 9 (star) Diego Barucco/Shutterstock.com; p. 9 (Venus) Luis Stortini Sabor aka CVADRAT/Shutterstock.com; p. 10 Hemera/Thinkstock.com; p. 12 Elenamiv/Shutterstock.com; p. 13 Rafael Pacheco/Shutterstock.com; p. 14 worldswildlifewonders/Shutterstock.com; p. 15 saicle/Shutterstock.com; p. 16 Santia/Shutterstock.com; p. 17 clearviewstock/Shutterstock.com; p. 18 Andrey Kekyalyaynen/Shutterstock.com; p. 19 Babek Tafreshi/Contributor/SSPL/SSPL via Getty Images; p. 20 MOHAMMED ABED/Staff/AFP/AFP/Getty Images; p. 21 © iStockphoto.com/jamesbenet; p. 22 © iStockphoto.com/Maica.

Library of Congress Cataloging-in-Publication Data

Hudson, Rachel, 1984-
 Objects in the sky / Rachel Hudson.
     p. cm. — (Exploring Earth and space)
 Includes index.
ISBN: 978-1-4488-8848-1 (pbk.)
6-pack ISBN: 978-1-4488-8849-8
ISBN: 978-1-4488-8578-7 (lib. bdg.)
1. Stars—Juvenile literature. 2. Planets—Juvenile literature. 3. Solar system—Juvenile literature. I. Title.
QB801.7.H83 2012
523—dc23

                    2012012255

Manufactured in the United States of America

CPSIA Compliance Information: Batch #WS12RC: For further information contact Rosen Publishing, New York, New York at 1-800-237-9932.

Word Count: 483

Contents

What's in the Sky?

Do you ever look up at the sky? There are a lot of cool things to see. The sky looks different during the day than it does at night.

During the day, the sky is big and blue. We see the sun and the clouds. At night, the sky is dark. We see the moon and the stars.

The sky changes because Earth spins in a circle. We see
different things as it turns. Most things in the sky
are far away from Earth. They're in outer space.

Outer space is really big. Many things in space are part of a solar system. A solar system is made of a star and the planets and moons that **orbit** it.

Planets

Our solar system has eight planets. A planet is a large object that moves around the sun. Earth is a planet. We can see some other planets when we look at the sky.

Venus from Earth

Venus from space

The easiest planet to see in the sky is Venus. Venus is the brightest planet in the night sky. From Earth, it can look white or even a little bit blue.

Mars is also easy to spot in the sky. Mars is red. This makes it different from all the other planets. Mars is brighter than all the stars in the sky.

Our Solar System

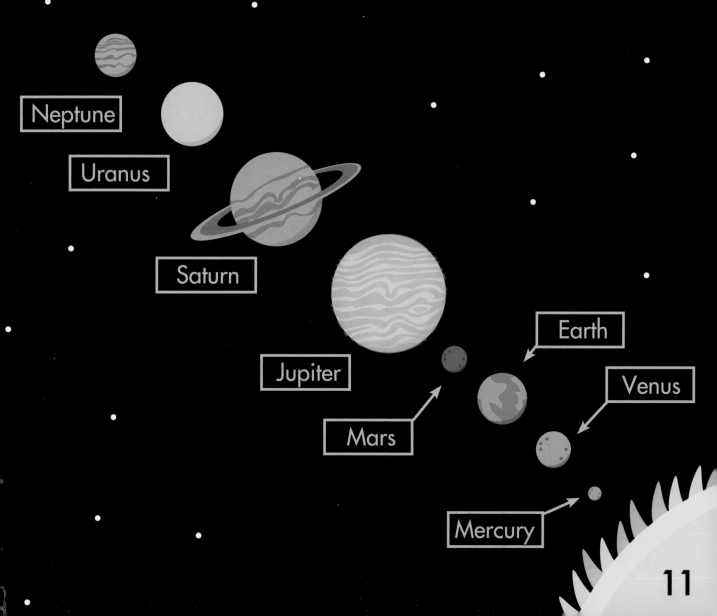

Neptune

Uranus

Saturn

Jupiter

Mars

Earth

Venus

Mercury

The Sun and Moon

We see the sun and the moon in the sky, too. The sun is big and very hot. Did you know that the sun is a star?

The sun comes up in the morning. This is called
a sunrise. At night, the sun goes away. This is called
a sunset. This happens because Earth spins.

The sun shines on the moon all day. At night, we see the moon because it **reflects** that light onto Earth. This is how the moon gives us light when it's dark outside.

The moon looks different on different days of the month. That's because it moves in a circle around Earth. It takes a whole month for the moon to finish its orbit.

Stars

We see stars at night, too. Stars make the sky look very pretty. Sometimes, we see **constellations**. The Big Dipper is a constellation.

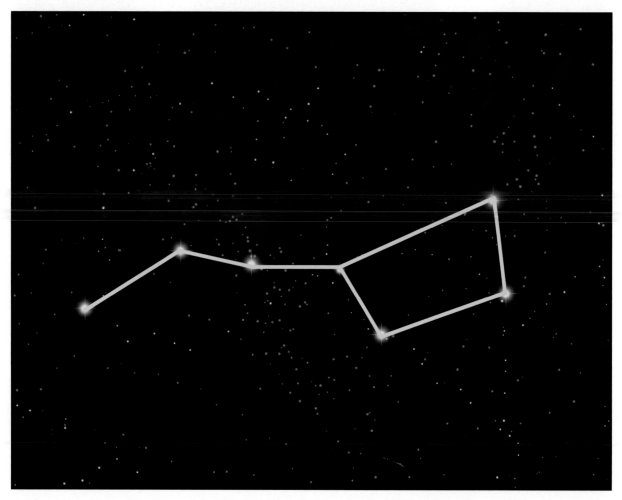

A long time ago, people used the stars as a guide.

The stars helped them figure out directions

when they were in new places.

Telescopes

We can see some things in the sky with our eyes,

but sometimes we need tools to help us.

One tool we use is a **telescope**.

Telescopes help us see things that are really far away.

Telescopes also make things look bigger.

A lot of people have telescopes in their backyard.

They look up into the sky for fun. There's a lot to see!

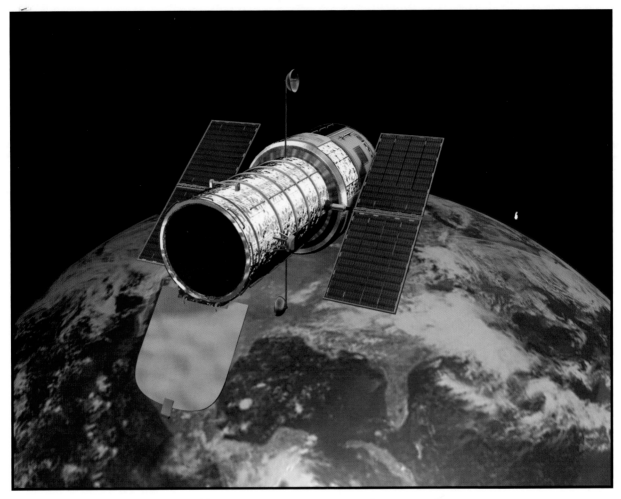

Some telescopes float in space. They take pictures
of planets and stars that we can't see from Earth.

It's fun to look at the sky. We see something new every day. What things do you see in the sky?

Glossary

constellation (kahn-stuh-LAY-shun) A group of stars that form a picture.

orbit (OHR-buht) To move in a circle around something. Also, the path of an object that moves in a circle around another object.

reflect (rih-FLEHKT) To throw back light.

telescope (TEH-luh-skohp) A tool used to see things that are far away.

Index

Due to the changing nature of Internet links, The Rosen Publishing Group, Inc., has developed an online list of websites related to the subject of this book. This site is updated regularly. Please use this link to access the list: www.powerkidslinks.com/ees/sky